The Giant Book of Spectacular Facts

by
Jake Jacobs

* * * * *

Published by Jake Jacobs

1.

Old New-Gate Prison is one of the oldest surviving penal institutions in the United States, dating back to the 18th century.

2.

It was originally established in 1773 as a copper mine by a group of investors led by John Viets.

3.

The copper mine at New-Gate was one of the first industrial mining operations in the American colonies.

4.

The mine was named "New-Gate" because it resembled the infamous Newgate Prison in London.

5.

In 1775, due to financial difficulties, the mine was converted into a colonial-era prison to house criminals.

6.

Old New-Gate Prison became Connecticut's first state prison and one of the first state prisons in the United States.

7.

The prison was constructed using a combination of stone and wood, and it featured cells carved directly into the rock.

8.

Prisoners at New-Gate were forced to work in the copper mine as part of their punishment.

9.

The mine's harsh conditions and the grueling labor made it a particularly brutal place to be incarcerated.

10.

Many prisoners died from the harsh conditions, disease, and accidents while working in the mine.

11.

In the 19th century, the prison was a major tourist attraction, drawing visitors interested in its history and eerie atmosphere.

12.

Notable visitors to Old New-Gate Prison included Mark Twain and Charles Dickens.

13.

Charles Dickens wrote about his visit to New-Gate Prison in his travel book "American Notes."

14.

The prison was abandoned in 1827 due to deteriorating conditions and a shift in the state's approach to incarceration.

15.

The site was later preserved and became a historic landmark, attracting visitors interested in its history and haunted reputation.

16.

Old New-Gate Prison is often referred to as one of the most haunted places in Connecticut.

17.

Over the years, there have been numerous reports of ghostly sightings and paranormal activity at the site.

18.

In the 20th century, the prison site underwent restoration efforts to preserve its historical significance.

19.

The State of Connecticut took ownership of the property and designated it as a state historical site.

20.

The site features guided tours that provide insights into the history of the prison, the copper mining operations, and the lives of the inmates.

21.

The mine shafts and tunnels at Old New-Gate Prison are considered some of the best-preserved examples of colonial mining in the United States.

22.

The prison's architecture and layout offer a unique glimpse into the conditions faced by prisoners during the colonial era.

23.

The site includes reconstructed gallows and a replica of a whipping post, providing a chilling reminder of the punishments inflicted on inmates.

24.

Visitors can explore the original cells carved into the rock and learn about the lives of prisoners who were confined there.

25.

Old New-Gate Prison was designated a National Historic Landmark in 1965.

26.

The prison site is managed by the State of Connecticut and is operated as a museum and educational center.

27.

The museum showcases artifacts, documents, and exhibits related to the prison's history and its transition from copper mine to penal institution.

28.

The prison's history is intertwined with the broader historical context of Connecticut's colonial and early statehood period.

29.

The site's historical significance extends beyond its use as a prison, encompassing the early mining industry in the American colonies.

30.

Old New-Gate Prison has been featured in documentaries and television shows focusing on historical and paranormal topics.

31.

The eerie and atmospheric nature of the prison site has made it a popular location for ghost hunting and paranormal investigations.

32.

The site's reputation as a haunted location has led to the production of books and articles exploring its supernatural legends.

33.

Visitors have reported hearing mysterious footsteps, disembodied voices, and unexplained sounds within the prison's confines.

34.

Some accounts suggest that the spirits of former inmates may still linger in the dark passages and cells of the prison.

35.

The prison's history and legends have inspired creative works, including literature, art, and local folklore.

36.

The surrounding landscape of Old New-Gate Prison is characterized by woodlands and picturesque scenery.

37.

The prison's location in the Farmington River Valley adds to its historical ambiance and the sense of isolation experienced by inmates.

38.

The site offers educational programs and events that explore various aspects of its history, from colonial mining to criminal justice.

39.

Old New-Gate Prison's significance as a historic site sheds light on the evolution of penal practices and attitudes toward punishment.

40.

The prison's preservation efforts have aimed to maintain the authenticity of its historical features and structures.

41.

The museum offers a glimpse into the lives of notable prisoners and their stories, contributing to the understanding of Connecticut's history.

42.

Some accounts suggest that Old New-Gate Prison played a role in shaping the penitentiary system in the United States.

43.

The site's history reflects the challenges faced by early colonists and the ways they adapted to their new environment.

44.

The prison's haunted reputation has attracted interest from paranormal enthusiasts, investigators, and thrill-seekers.

45.

The museum's exhibits provide insights into the lives of the guards and staff who worked at the prison throughout its history.

46.

Old New-Gate Prison serves as a reminder of the hardships and struggles faced by individuals during the colonial era.

47.

The site's historical significance extends beyond its regional impact to offer insights into broader themes of justice and incarceration.

48.

The prison's complex history is reflected in its changing roles as a copper mine, a colonial jail, a tourist attraction, and a historic site.

49.

Old New-Gate Prison's unique architecture and layout make it a valuable resource for architectural historians and preservationists.

50.

The preservation of Old New-Gate Prison ensures that future generations can learn about its multifaceted history and the experiences of those who lived and worked there.

51.

The Old State House was completed in 1796 and served as the Connecticut State House until 1878.

52.

It is one of the oldest state houses in the United States that is still standing and in use.

53.

The building's architectural style is Georgian, characterized by its symmetrical design and red brick exterior.

54.

The Old State House is located in the heart of Hartford's historic district, surrounded by modern buildings.

55.

The building's design was influenced by the works of renowned architect Charles Bulfinch, known for his contributions to American neoclassical architecture.

56.

The Old State House was constructed at a cost of $63,500, which was considered substantial at the time.

57.

The building's original purpose was to house the legislative and executive branches of Connecticut's state government.

58.

It was also used as a courthouse, hosting various legal proceedings and trials throughout its history.

59.

The building's front façade features a central portico supported by four Doric columns, creating a grand entrance.

60.

Inside, the Old State House has a large central hall with a marble floor and a grand staircase leading to the second floor.

61.

The second-floor chamber, known as the Senate Chamber, was where the Connecticut State Senate met.

62.

The Old State House was the site of numerous historic events, including the Amistad trial in 1839.

63.

The Amistad trial centered on a group of enslaved Africans who rebelled against their captors on the ship Amistad. The trial was a pivotal moment in the fight against slavery.

64.

The trial's proceedings took place in the Old State House's courtroom, attracting national and international attention.

65.

The Old State House also hosted a variety of public gatherings, including political speeches, lectures, and public meetings.

66.

The building's historical significance led to its designation as a National Historic Landmark in 1960.

67.

The Old State House has undergone multiple renovations and restorations to preserve its historical integrity.

68.

The building's exterior features an iconic gold-domed cupola, which serves as a symbol of Connecticut's early history.

69.

The cupola was reconstructed in the mid-19th century after the original was damaged by a tornado.

70.

Inside the Old State House, visitors can explore exhibits that highlight Connecticut's history and its role in American democracy.

71.

The building houses a collection of artifacts, documents, and historical displays related to the state's history.

72.

The Old State House is known for its "Charter Oak Chair," a symbol of Connecticut's colonial history.

73.

The Charter Oak Chair is said to be made from wood salvaged from the famous Charter Oak tree, under which Connecticut's colonial charter was famously hidden to prevent its confiscation by British authorities.

74.

The Old State House is open to the public for guided tours, allowing visitors to learn about its rich history and architectural significance.

75.

The building's location makes it a popular tourist destination in Hartford, attracting history enthusiasts and sightseers alike.

76.

The Old State House's central location has also made it a gathering place for public events, rallies, and celebrations.

77.

The building has witnessed significant political debates and discussions that have shaped Connecticut's history.

78.

The Old State House's legacy as a seat of government makes it an important part of the state's political heritage.

79.

The building's significance extends beyond Connecticut, as it represents the principles of representative democracy and civic engagement.

80.

The Old State House has been featured in various films, television shows, and documentaries highlighting its historical importance.

81.

The building's architecture and design continue to influence public buildings and state houses across the country.

82.

The Old State House has served as a symbol of resilience, having survived natural disasters, changes in government, and modern urban development.

83.

The building's preservation efforts are supported by organizations dedicated to maintaining its historical and cultural value.

84.

The Old State House's exhibits cover a wide range of topics, from Connecticut's colonial beginnings to its role in the American Revolution and beyond.

85.

The site's educational programs cater to students and visitors interested in learning about Connecticut's history and its impact on the nation.

86.

The Old State House also hosts special events, lectures, and temporary exhibitions that explore various aspects of the state's heritage.

87.

The building's grand architecture and historic charm make it a popular venue for weddings, receptions, and private events.

88.

The Old State House's guided tours provide insights into the lives of Connecticut's early leaders and the historical context in which they operated.

89.

The site's historical significance has led to ongoing efforts to preserve and maintain its structural integrity.

90.

The Old State House continues to be an important destination for school groups, tourists, and local residents seeking a connection to Connecticut's past.

91.

The building's role in shaping the state's laws, government, and culture has left a lasting impact on Connecticut's identity.

92.

The Old State House's preservation serves as a reminder of the importance of historical landmarks in connecting people to their heritage.

93.

The building's connection to significant events in American history underscores its relevance as a cultural and educational resource.

94.

The Old State House stands as a testament to the generations of Connecticut citizens who have contributed to the state's growth and development.

95.

The site's staff and volunteers work diligently to provide accurate and engaging historical information to visitors of all ages.

96.

The Old State House's legacy as a place of civic engagement and political discourse continues to inspire discussions about democracy and governance.

97.

The building's architecture reflects the neoclassical style prevalent during the late 18th century, blending symmetry, proportion, and classical motifs.

98.

The Old State House's exterior brickwork and design showcase the craftsmanship of the artisans who constructed it over two centuries ago.

99.

The site's significance has led to collaborations with other historical institutions, scholars, and organizations dedicated to preserving history.

100.

The Old State House remains a cherished landmark that bridges the past and the present, offering visitors a glimpse into Connecticut's history and its role in shaping the nation's democratic ideals.

101.

The Harbour Porpoise (Phocoena phocoena) is one of the smallest and most widely distributed cetacean species.

102.

They are also known as common porpoises and are found in coastal and continental shelf waters of the Northern Hemisphere.

103.

Harbour Porpoises have a sleek and streamlined body, with a rounded forehead and a relatively small triangular dorsal fin.

104.

They are known for their characteristic rolling motion when swimming at the surface, often showing their back and dorsal fin.

105.

Harbour Porpoises have a dark gray to black coloration on their upper side and a lighter gray or white underside.

106.

These porpoises are social animals and are often found in small groups known as pods.

107.

Harbour Porpoises are primarily solitary feeders, but they occasionally hunt in groups to exploit a school of fish.

108.

They are skilled hunters and mainly feed on small fish and squid, using echolocation to locate their prey.

109.

Echolocation is a biological sonar system that Harbour Porpoises use to navigate and locate prey by emitting high-frequency clicks and listening to the echoes.

110.

Harbour Porpoises have a relatively short lifespan, with most individuals living around 10-15 years.

111.

The size of Harbour Porpoises varies depending on their location, but they generally reach lengths of 4.6 to 6 feet (1.4 to 1.8 meters).

112.

Adult Harbour Porpoises can weigh between 110 to 150 pounds (50 to 68 kilograms).

113.

These porpoises have a relatively fast swimming speed and can reach speeds of up to 25 mph (40 km/h).

114.

Harbour Porpoises are known for their acrobatic behaviors, often leaping out of the water and riding in the bow waves of boats.

115.

They have a unique breathing pattern, typically exhaling before diving and inhaling at the surface.

116.

Harbour Porpoises have a low reproductive rate, with females giving birth to a single calf every one to two years.

117.

The calf is born tail-first in order to prevent drowning, and mothers are highly attentive to their offspring.

118.

Newborn Harbour Porpoises are about 2.3 to 3.3 feet (70 to 100 cm) long and weigh around 8.8 to 17.6 pounds (4 to 8 kg).

119.

These porpoises have a wide distribution, being found in both the Atlantic and Pacific Oceans.

120.

Their range spans from the Arctic to the subtropics, and they are commonly sighted in coastal waters.

121.

Harbour Porpoises are known to migrate seasonally, moving to colder waters in the summer and warmer waters in the winter.

122.

They are considered shy and elusive animals, often avoiding boats and human interaction.

123.

The main threats to Harbour Porpoises include bycatch in fishing gear, habitat degradation, pollution, and noise pollution from human activities.

124.

Noise pollution from boat traffic and underwater construction can interfere with their echolocation and communication.

125.

Harbour Porpoises are protected under various international agreements and laws, such as the Marine Mammal Protection Act in the United States.

126.

In some regions, Harbour Porpoises have been hunted for their meat and oil, but hunting is now largely prohibited.

127.

The IUCN classifies Harbour Porpoises as a species of "Least Concern" due to their relatively stable population size.

128.

Porpoises and dolphins are often confused, but porpoises have shorter beaks, flatter teeth, and a different body shape compared to dolphins.

129.

Unlike dolphins, porpoises don't have a pronounced beak, and their teeth are spade-shaped rather than conical.

130.

Harbour Porpoises have a complex communication system that includes clicks, whistles, and body movements.

131.

They use these vocalizations to communicate with each other, locate prey, and navigate their environment.

132.

Porpoises are known for their agility and ability to navigate through complex underwater environments with ease.

133.

The oldest known Harbour Porpoise reached an age of around 23 years.

134.

Harbour Porpoises are known to leap out of the water, sometimes performing somersaults or spins in the air.

135.

Despite their small size, Harbour Porpoises are known for their strong swimming and energetic behavior.

136.

The conservation status of Harbour Porpoises can vary by region, with some populations facing greater threats than others.

137.

In some areas, such as the Baltic Sea, Harbour Porpoise populations are considered endangered due to factors like bycatch.

138.

Harbour Porpoises are known to exhibit curiosity toward boats, occasionally approaching vessels to investigate.

139.

They have been observed engaging in social behaviors such as synchronized swimming and group hunting.

140.

The name "porpoise" is believed to have originated from the Latin word "porcopiscus," which means "pig fish."

141.

Harbour Porpoises have been depicted in various cultures' folklore and art, often symbolizing grace and freedom.

142.

The Harbour Porpoise was featured on the reverse side of the Canadian 10-cent coin from 1937 to 1952.

143.

Researchers use photo-identification techniques to study individual Harbour Porpoises, recognizing them by unique markings on their dorsal fins.

144.

In some regions, Harbour Porpoises face threats from marine traffic collisions, especially in areas with heavy shipping lanes.

145.

Efforts are being made to reduce human impacts on Harbour Porpoises by implementing speed limits in areas with high porpoise activity.

146.

There are ongoing conservation projects focused on improving fishing practices to minimize bycatch of Harbour Porpoises.

147.

In some locations, Harbour Porpoise-watching tours are offered to educate the public about these animals and their conservation needs.

148.

Harbour Porpoises are known to be quite resilient and adaptable to changes in their environment.

149.

Their survival is crucial to maintaining the health of marine ecosystems, as they play a role in controlling prey populations.

150.

The study and conservation of Harbour Porpoises provide valuable insights into the overall health of marine environments and the impacts of human activities on aquatic ecosystems.

151.

The Harp Seal (Pagophilus groenlandicus) is a marine mammal that belongs to the family Phocidae, commonly known as "true seals."

152.

They are also known as saddleback seals due to the harp-like markings on the backs of adult seals.

153.

Harp Seals are found in the North Atlantic and Arctic Oceans, particularly in the colder regions of Canada, Greenland, and Russia.

154.

These seals have a distinct coloration, with a silver-gray to black dorsal side and a lighter gray or white ventral side.

155.

Harp Seals are well adapted to cold environments, with a thick layer of blubber and dense fur to insulate their bodies.

156.

Adult Harp Seals have a unique pattern of black markings on their backs that resembles a harp or a horseshoe.

157.

Harp Seals have large, black eyes that are well adapted to low light conditions in their Arctic habitat.

158.

The scientific name "Pagophilus groenlandicus" translates to "ice-loving seal of Greenland," reflecting their affinity for icy waters.

159.

These seals are excellent swimmers and divers, capable of diving to depths of up to 600 feet (180 meters) and staying submerged for around 15 minutes.

160.

Harp Seals feed primarily on a diet of small fish, crustaceans, and invertebrates found in the cold waters they inhabit.

161.

They have specialized teeth for catching and gripping their slippery prey.

162.

Female Harp Seals usually give birth to a single pup each year, typically on pack ice in late February to March.

163.

The pups are born with a fluffy white coat called "lanugo," which helps them stay warm in their icy environment.

164.

Harp Seal mothers are known for their strong maternal instincts and will fiercely protect their pups from predators.

165.

Pups are nursed for about 12 to 14 days, during which they gain weight rapidly.

166.

After the nursing period, the pups molt their white fur and develop a short, gray pelage similar to that of adult seals.

167.

Harp Seals communicate with each other using various vocalizations, including grunts, barks, and growls.

168.

In some regions, Harp Seals are hunted for their fur and blubber, primarily for their oil content.

169.

The hunting of Harp Seals has been a subject of controversy and international attention due to animal rights concerns.

170.

Harp Seals are classified as "Least Concern" by the IUCN, as their population appears to be stable.

171.

Climate change and reduction in sea ice due to warming temperatures could potentially impact Harp Seal populations by affecting their breeding and feeding habitats.

172.

Harp Seals have a relatively short life span, with males typically living around 20 to 30 years and females 30 to 35 years.

173.

The seals spend much of their lives at sea, only coming ashore during the breeding season.

174.

Harp Seals have specialized nasal passages that help them conserve heat and moisture while breathing in the cold, dry air of their Arctic habitat.

175.

The annual migration of Harp Seals between their breeding and feeding grounds can cover distances of thousands of kilometers.

176.

The diet of Harp Seals changes with their age and location. Young seals mainly eat shrimp-like krill, while adults diversify their diet to include more fish.

177.

Harp Seals are known to bask on ice floes and haul out on rocky shores to rest.

178.

The diet and behavior of Harp Seals are influenced by the seasonal availability of prey species and ice cover.

179.

Male Harp Seals are larger than females and have a characteristic "saddle" marking on their back.

180.

Harp Seal pups are born with blue eyes, which gradually change to a darker color as they mature.

181.

Conservation efforts focus on protecting Harp Seal habitats and minimizing human disturbances, particularly during the sensitive breeding season.

182.

Harp Seals play a crucial role in the marine food web by controlling the populations of their prey species.

183.

The Harp Seal population is estimated to be around 7 to 9 million individuals.

184.

Harp Seals are known to gather in large groups on ice floes, a behavior known as "hauling out."

185.

The seals' ability to move effortlessly between ice and water is essential for their survival in the Arctic ecosystem.

186.

Harp Seal milk is highly nutritious and contains a high fat content to help pups quickly gain weight.

187.

Harp Seals are known for their playful behavior, often engaging in activities like surfing on ice floes and interacting with each other.

188.

The primary predators of Harp Seals include polar bears and killer whales, especially young pups that are vulnerable on the ice.

189.

Harp Seals are known to migrate long distances in search of food, often following the movement of their prey species.

190.

The population dynamics of Harp Seals are closely linked to the availability of sea ice, which provides breeding and resting sites.

191.

Female Harp Seals reach sexual maturity at around 5 to 7 years of age, while males reach maturity later, at 7 to 9 years.

192.

Harp Seals have been a subject of study for scientists to understand various aspects of marine ecology and climate change effects.

193.

The Harp Seal's distinctive markings make them relatively easy to identify individually in the wild, aiding researchers in tracking their movements and behavior.

194.

Harp Seals have been observed using their flippers to push ice floes aside, creating breathing holes in the ice.

195.

The annual arrival of Harp Seals in certain areas for breeding is a natural spectacle that draws attention from tourists and wildlife enthusiasts.

196.

In some cultures, Harp Seals hold cultural significance and are often depicted in art and folklore.

197.

Harp Seals have a specialized vascular system called the "rete mirabile" that helps maintain their body temperature even in cold water.

198.

Harp Seals are known for their distinctive "clapping" vocalizations, which they produce by slapping their flippers against the water.

199.

The "harp" or "saddle" marking on the back of Harp Seals is most pronounced in younger individuals and may fade as they age.

200.

Understanding the ecology and behaviors of Harp Seals is essential for effective conservation efforts and maintaining the health of Arctic marine ecosystems.

201.

Kaiser Permanente is one of the largest managed care organizations in the United States, providing healthcare services to millions of members.

202.

The organization was founded by industrialist Henry J. Kaiser and physician Sidney R. Garfield in 1945.

203.

The concept of Kaiser Permanente originated during World War II when Kaiser was building ships for the U.S. Maritime Commission and Garfield provided medical care to workers.

204.

The first Kaiser Permanente medical facility was established in the Mojave Desert, California, to provide healthcare for workers building the Colorado River Aqueduct.

205.

The name "Permanente" was chosen to reflect the comprehensive, continuous, and integrated care that the organization aimed to provide.

206.

Kaiser Permanente's model was based on the idea of prepaid healthcare, where members paid a fixed monthly fee for access to medical services.

207.

The organization's first hospital was established in Oakland, California, in 1942, to serve workers building ships for the war effort.

208.

The founding principles of Kaiser Permanente included a focus on preventive care, community health, and affordable access to medical services.

209.

Kaiser Permanente's integrated model of care includes hospitals, medical offices, and health plans, all under one umbrella.

210.

The organization's first health plan was created for workers at the Richmond Field Hospital in California in 1942.

211.

Kaiser Permanente played a pioneering role in promoting health insurance coverage for all employees, setting a precedent for employer-sponsored healthcare.

212.

The Permanente Medical Group (TPMG) was established to oversee the medical care provided within the Kaiser Permanente system.

213.

Kaiser Permanente was among the first healthcare organizations to adopt electronic medical records and health information technology.

214.

In 1951, Kaiser Permanente established its first health plan for non-employees, expanding its services beyond the workforce.

215.

The organization's focus on preventive care and wellness programs has contributed to its reputation for proactive health management.

216.

Kaiser Permanente is known for its commitment to evidence-based medicine and continuous quality improvement.

217.

The organization has been recognized for its efforts in reducing health disparities and improving access to care in underserved communities.

218.

In the 1960s, Kaiser Permanente expanded its operations beyond California, establishing health plans in other states.

219.

Kaiser Permanente played a significant role in advocating for the development and implementation of the Medicare and Medicaid programs.

220.

The organization's commitment to affordable healthcare led to the creation of health maintenance organizations (HMOs) as a viable healthcare model.

221.

Kaiser Permanente's emphasis on preventive care and healthy lifestyle choices has led to various wellness initiatives for members.

222.

The organization has been involved in medical research, contributing to advancements in healthcare practices and treatments.

223.

Kaiser Permanente has its own research institute, known for conducting studies on population health, disease prevention, and treatment effectiveness.

224.

The organization has been recognized for its efforts in improving patient safety and implementing innovative healthcare technologies.

225.

Kaiser Permanente has been a pioneer in using telemedicine and digital health platforms to enhance patient access and convenience.

226.

In 2006, Kaiser Permanente established the Garfield Innovation Center, dedicated to designing and testing innovative healthcare solutions.

227.

The organization's commitment to environmental sustainability has led to various initiatives to reduce its carbon footprint and promote eco-friendly practices.

228.

Kaiser Permanente is known for its strong emphasis on patient-centered care, involving patients in treatment decisions and care planning.

229.

The organization has been recognized for its cultural competency and efforts to provide equitable care for diverse populations.

230.

Kaiser Permanente's involvement in community health extends beyond clinical care, including education and outreach programs.

231.

The organization's focus on preventive care and early detection has contributed to improved outcomes for chronic conditions.

232.

Kaiser Permanente's coordinated care model involves collaboration among physicians, specialists, nurses, and other healthcare professionals.

233.

The organization's commitment to affordable healthcare has led to innovative cost-saving measures and efficient resource allocation.

234.

Kaiser Permanente's integrated electronic health record system allows for seamless sharing of patient information among care providers.

235.

The organization has received recognition for its efforts in improving patient satisfaction and patient engagement.

236.

Kaiser Permanente's commitment to transparency is evident through public reporting of quality measures and outcomes data.

237.

The organization has been a leader in promoting vaccination campaigns and public health initiatives.

238.

Kaiser Permanente's involvement in medical education and training has contributed to a skilled healthcare workforce.

239.

The organization's founder, Henry J. Kaiser, also had a significant impact on other industries, including shipbuilding and construction.

240.

Kaiser Permanente has partnered with various academic institutions and research organizations to advance medical knowledge.

241.

The organization has been at the forefront of adopting alternative payment models to improve care coordination and reduce costs.

242.

Kaiser Permanente's commitment to preventive care aligns with its focus on population health management.

243.

The organization's comprehensive approach to healthcare includes addressing social determinants of health that impact patients' well-being.

244.

Kaiser Permanente has received numerous awards for its commitment to patient safety, quality improvement, and healthcare innovation.

245.

The organization's research has contributed to advancements in areas such as cancer treatment, chronic disease management, and patient care delivery.

246.

Kaiser Permanente has a strong tradition of community involvement, supporting local health initiatives and community events.

247.

The organization's success has led to its expansion into international markets, sharing its healthcare expertise with other countries.

248.

Kaiser Permanente has consistently ranked among the top healthcare providers in terms of quality and patient satisfaction.

249.

The organization's dedication to continuous improvement is evident through its participation in initiatives to reduce healthcare costs while maintaining high standards of care.

250.

Kaiser Permanente's history reflects its commitment to providing accessible, affordable, and high-quality healthcare services to its members and communities.

251.

Zillow was founded in 2006 by Rich Barton and Lloyd Frink as a real estate and rental marketplace.

252.

The company's name "Zillow" is a combination of the words "zillion" (indicating a large quantity) and "pillow" (representing home comfort).

253.

Zillow initially launched as a website offering estimated home values, known as "Zestimates," for properties across the United States.

254.

Zestimates are calculated using algorithms that consider various factors such as property location, size, features, and comparable sales.

255.

Zillow's online platform provides users with a wealth of information, including property listings, rental listings, mortgage rates, and more.

256.

In addition to residential properties, Zillow also includes commercial real estate listings on its platform.

257.

Zillow's Zestimate feature has sparked both praise and controversy, with some homeowners feeling that their home's value was inaccurately estimated.

258.

Over the years, Zillow has expanded its services to include tools for buyers, sellers, renters, and real estate professionals.

259.

The company's "Premier Agent" program allows real estate agents to advertise on Zillow and connect with potential clients.

260.

Zillow offers a "Make Me Move" feature that allows homeowners to list their properties at a certain price, even if they're not officially on the market.

261.

Zillow's "Instant Offers" program enables homeowners to receive offers from investors and potential buyers for their properties.

262.

In 2015, Zillow acquired Trulia, another major online real estate marketplace, which allowed the company to strengthen its market position.

263.

The Zillow Group, which includes Zillow, Trulia, and other brands, is one of the largest online real estate platforms in the world.

264.

Zillow's mobile app has gained immense popularity, allowing users to search for properties, access Zestimates, and find real estate agents on the go.

265.

The company introduced a feature called "Zillow 3D Home" that lets users create virtual tours of their properties using a smartphone.

266.

Zillow's "Rent Zestimates" provide estimated rental prices for homes and apartments, helping renters make informed decisions.

267.

Zillow has a "Rent Index" that tracks rental price changes in various cities and neighborhoods over time.

268.

In addition to its U.S. operations, Zillow expanded to Canada in 2018, starting with the launch of Zillow.com in select markets.

269.

Zillow Offers is a program that allows homeowners to sell their homes directly to Zillow, offering convenience and speed in the selling process.

270.

The company's Zillow Home Loans division offers mortgage services to homebuyers, making the home financing process more streamlined.

271.

Zillow's "Premier Broker" program connects real estate agents with buyers and sellers, aiming to enhance the real estate transaction experience.

272.

Zillow's "Home Report" feature provides detailed information about a property's history, including previous sales, tax assessments, and more.

273.

The company has been involved in various legal disputes related to the accuracy of Zestimates and listing data.

274.

Zillow has also faced criticism from some real estate professionals who feel that the company's practices could disrupt traditional real estate models.

275.

The "Zillow Prize" competition was launched to encourage data scientists and researchers to improve the accuracy of Zestimates.

276.

Zillow has an annual event called "Zillow Premier Agent Forum," where real estate professionals can network and learn about industry trends.

277.

The company's "Zillow Academy" offers training and educational resources for real estate agents looking to enhance their skills.

278.

Zillow's "Zillow Offers" program allows homeowners to request a cash offer for their property, providing a potential alternative to the traditional selling process.

279.

Zillow's platform includes a feature that allows users to save and track their favorite listings, receive alerts about price changes, and more.

280.

The company's "Zillow Research" division produces reports on housing trends, affordability, and other real estate-related topics.

281.

Zillow's CEO, Rich Barton, previously co-founded Expedia and Glassdoor, showcasing his experience in the technology and e-commerce sectors.

282.

Zillow's "Walk Score" feature rates the walkability of neighborhoods based on proximity to amenities, services, and public transportation.

283.

Zillow provides aerial images of properties using its "Zillow Aerial View" feature, helping users get a better sense of the surrounding area.

284.

The company introduced "Zillow Offers for Homebuilders," allowing new construction home sellers to connect with Zillow Offers.

285.

Zillow's "Premier Agent Direct" program enables agents to advertise on Zillow through targeted ads on Facebook and Instagram.

286.

Zillow's "Zillow Rental Manager" allows property managers and landlords to list their rental properties on Zillow and other platforms.

287.

The company's "Zillow Rental Manager" also includes tools for tenant screening and lease management.

288.

Zillow has expanded its services to include property management software called "Buildium" for landlords and property managers.

289.

The company's "Zillow Group Mortgages" division offers various mortgage products and services to homebuyers.

290.

Zillow's "Zillow Offers for Sellers" program aims to simplify the home selling process, providing sellers with more options.

291.

Zillow has a strong commitment to corporate social responsibility and has been involved in initiatives to support affordable housing and disaster relief efforts.

292.

Zillow's "Zillow Premier Agent App" is designed specifically for real estate agents to manage leads and communicate with clients.

293.

The company's "Zillow Digs" feature offers inspiration and ideas for home remodeling and design projects.

294.

Zillow's "Ownership Dashboard" provides homeowners with insights into their home's value, equity, and other financial aspects.

295.

Zillow has a "Seller Dashboard" feature that gives sellers updates on their listing's performance and offers.

296.

The company's "Zillow Home Loans" division offers a streamlined mortgage application process for homebuyers.

297.

Zillow's "Zillow 360" program allows real estate agents to create virtual tours of properties using 360-degree panoramic photos.

298.

Zillow's "Zillow Tech Connect: Bridge API" allows agents to seamlessly integrate Zillow data into their own applications and websites.

299.

The company's "Zillow Innovation Lab" explores emerging technologies and concepts that could shape the future of real estate.

300.

Zillow's continued growth and innovation have solidified its position as a major player in the real estate industry, providing consumers with valuable tools and resources for navigating the housing market.

301.

The Captain Nathaniel B. Palmer House is located in Stonington, Connecticut, USA.

302.

The house was built in 1852 and is a Greek Revival-style structure.

303.

It is named after Captain Nathaniel Brown Palmer, a sea captain and explorer who is known for discovering Antarctica.

304.

Captain Nathaniel B. Palmer was born in Stonington in 1799.

305.

The house was constructed for Captain Palmer's sister, Betsey T. Palmer.

306.

The house was originally used as a private residence.

307.

The Captain Nathaniel B. Palmer House is listed on the National Register of Historic Places.

308.

The house is an example of the Greek Revival architecture popular in the mid-19th century.

309.

It features a symmetrical facade, gabled roof, and columns characteristic of the Greek Revival style.

310.

The house is made of wood and has a clapboard exterior.

311.

The property surrounding the house includes a garden and lawn area.

312.

The Captain Nathaniel B. Palmer House has a historical marker that provides information about its significance.

313.

Captain Nathaniel B. Palmer is often credited with being one of the first Americans to see Antarctica in 1820.

314.

He discovered Antarctica while commanding the sloop Hero, during a sealing and exploration expedition.

315.

The discovery of Antarctica is significant in the history of exploration and geographic knowledge.

316.

Captain Palmer's expeditions helped contribute to a better understanding of the Southern Hemisphere.

317.

The house has changed hands multiple times since its construction.

318.

It has undergone restoration efforts to preserve its historical integrity.

319.

The house provides insight into the maritime history of Stonington and its connection to exploration.

320.

Captain Nathaniel B. Palmer's legacy continues to be celebrated in the region and beyond.

321.

The house has been recognized for its architectural and historical significance.

322.

It serves as a reminder of the seafaring heritage of Stonington and its residents.

323.

The Captain Nathaniel B. Palmer House is a popular destination for history enthusiasts and visitors interested in maritime history.

324.

The house is located within walking distance of other historic sites in Stonington, making it part of a broader historical context.

325.

Stonington is known for its picturesque coastal setting and charming New England architecture.

326.

The house's interior features period-appropriate furnishings and decor that offer a glimpse into the past.

327.

Captain Nathaniel B. Palmer's exploration of Antarctica was a significant achievement in the Age of Discovery.

328.

The house's design reflects the architectural trends of the mid-19th century, including its use of columns and pediments.

329.

The house's location near the water highlights its connection to Stonington's maritime history.

330.

Captain Palmer's voyages contributed to expanding knowledge of the world's geography and natural resources.

331.

The Captain Nathaniel B. Palmer House stands as a tribute to the curiosity and courage of explorers during that era.

332.

The house's preservation efforts aim to ensure that future generations can learn from and appreciate its historical significance.

333.

The property's garden area may feature plantings that were common during the mid-19th century.

334.

The Captain Nathaniel B. Palmer House serves as a reminder of the achievements of individuals from small coastal communities.

335.

The house's location in Stonington Harbor reflects the town's historical ties to maritime commerce and exploration.

336.

The Captain Nathaniel B. Palmer House is an example of how architecture can reflect the cultural values and aspirations of a community.

337.

The house's historical marker provides a concise overview of Captain Palmer's accomplishments and legacy.

338.

The building's design showcases the influence of Greek architectural styles on American domestic architecture.

339.

Stonington's maritime heritage is celebrated through events, exhibits, and attractions such as the Captain Nathaniel B. Palmer House.

340.

The house's history contributes to the broader narrative of American exploration and expansion.

341.

The Captain Nathaniel B. Palmer House offers a tangible connection to the past, allowing visitors to step back in time.

342.

The house may feature artifacts and exhibits related to Captain Palmer and the Age of Exploration.

343.

The preservation of the Captain Nathaniel B. Palmer House is a collaborative effort involving local organizations and historical societies.

344.

The house's significance extends beyond its walls, influencing the community's sense of identity and history.

345.

The Captain Nathaniel B. Palmer House is a testament to the spirit of adventure and discovery that characterized the 19th century.

346.

Captain Palmer's exploration of Antarctica laid the groundwork for further scientific research in the region.

347.

The house's architectural details, such as its pilasters and entablature, showcase the attention to design during its construction.

348.

The house's location provides scenic views of the harbor and surrounding landscape.

349.

The Captain Nathaniel B. Palmer House is an integral part of the fabric of Stonington's historical district.

350.

Visiting the Captain Nathaniel B. Palmer House allows individuals to connect with history and learn about the achievements of a notable explorer.

351.

The Portland Brownstone Quarries are located in Portland, Connecticut, USA.

352.

The quarries are renowned for producing high-quality brownstone, a type of sandstone with a distinctive reddish-brown color.

353.

Brownstone from these quarries was widely used in the construction of buildings in the 19th century.

354.

The quarries played a pivotal role in shaping the architectural landscape of cities like New York City and Boston.

355.

The first quarry in Portland opened in the late 1600s, making it one of the oldest quarrying areas in the United States.

356.

The geological conditions in Portland were ideal for the formation of brownstone deposits.

357.

Brownstone from these quarries was characterized by its durability, workability, and aesthetic appeal.

358.

The quarries operated during the 18th and 19th centuries, producing stone for numerous buildings across the country.

359.

One of the most famous structures built using Portland brownstone is the iconic Brooklyn Bridge in New York City.

360.

Other notable buildings featuring Portland brownstone include parts of the New York Public Library and the Boston Athenaeum.

361.

The brownstone was highly valued for its warm color, ease of carving, and resistance to weathering.

362.

Quarried blocks of brownstone were used for building facades, lintels, cornices, and other decorative elements.

363.

The use of Portland brownstone became popular during the Victorian era, as it complemented the ornate architectural styles of the time.

364.

The quarries experienced a peak in production during the mid-19th century due to the growing demand for brownstone.

365.

The transportation of brownstone from Portland to major cities was facilitated by riverboats and later by railroads.

366.

The brownstone industry in Portland created jobs and economic opportunities for the local community.

367.

The quarries also led to the growth of associated industries such as stonecutting and masonry.

368.

The quarrying process involved drilling holes, inserting explosives, and then breaking the stone into manageable blocks.

369.

As the demand for brownstone increased, many quarries expanded their operations to meet the needs of builders.

370.

The quarries were labor-intensive environments, with workers using hand tools and basic machinery to extract the stone.

371.

The brownstone was used not only for commercial buildings but also for private residences and churches.

372.

The decline of the brownstone industry began in the late 19th century as architectural tastes shifted and new materials became popular.

373.

The introduction of steel-framed construction and new construction methods reduced the need for massive stone blocks.

374.

Urban development and expansion also led to the exhaustion of brownstone resources in some quarries.

375.

The quarries faced challenges such as competition from other stone sources and economic fluctuations.

376.

Despite the decline of the industry, many historic buildings featuring Portland brownstone still stand as a testament to its enduring quality.

377.

Preservation efforts have focused on restoring and maintaining historic brownstone structures.

378.

Brownstone continues to be valued for its aesthetic appeal and historical significance in architecture.

379.

The Portland Brownstone Quarries have been recognized as a National Historic Landmark.

380.

Visitors to the quarries can see remnants of the quarrying process, including exposed brownstone walls and quarry pits.

381.

The quarries offer insights into the craftsmanship and labor that went into producing this unique building material.

382.

In recent years, there has been a renewed interest in using Portland brownstone for restoration and historic preservation projects.

383.

The brownstone industry's legacy has left an indelible mark on the built environment of many American cities.

384.

The quarries also played a role in shaping the culture and history of the local community in Portland.

385.

Portland brownstone became a symbol of architectural elegance and sophistication during its heyday.

386.

The quarries have been featured in documentaries, books, and articles exploring the history of American architecture and construction.

387.

Efforts have been made to document the stories and experiences of the quarry workers who contributed to the industry's success.

388.

The Portland Brownstone Quarries stand as a reminder of the interconnectedness between natural resources, craftsmanship, and design.

389.

The durability of brownstone has allowed historic structures to withstand the test of time and weathering.

390.

Brownstone buildings continue to captivate and inspire architects, historians, and the general public.

391.

The Portland Brownstone Quarries represent a time when natural resources directly shaped the urban landscape.

392.

The quarries' impact on architecture can still be seen in the rich architectural heritage of cities where brownstone was used.

393.

The cultural significance of Portland brownstone extends beyond its functional role in construction.

394.

The quarries' history provides a window into the economic and social dynamics of the 19th century.

395.

Preservationists and historians work to ensure that the legacy of the Portland Brownstone Quarries is not forgotten.

396.

The combination of manual labor, technology, and artistic expression in brownstone architecture highlights a unique period in American history.

397.

Brownstone buildings were often adorned with intricate carvings and ornamentation.

398.

The color of the stone evolved over time due to weathering and exposure to environmental factors.

399.

The Portland Brownstone Quarries have become a source of inspiration for architects seeking to integrate historical materials into modern designs.

400.

Visiting the Portland Brownstone Quarries provides an opportunity to reflect on the intersection of natural resources, architecture, and cultural heritage.

401.

The Hazel Dormouse (Muscardinus avellanarius) is also known as the common dormouse or the common hazel dormouse.

402.

It is a small rodent belonging to the family Gliridae, which includes several species of dormice.

403.

The dormouse's name "Muscardinus" is derived from the Latin words "mus," meaning mouse, and "cardinus," meaning hazel.

404.

Hazel dormice are widely distributed across Europe, including parts of the United Kingdom, and parts of Asia, from the Ural Mountains to Japan.

405.

They are known for their adorable appearance, with large eyes and a fluffy tail.

406.

The Hazel Dormouse has a rotund body covered in dense fur, which helps to insulate it against cold temperatures.

407.

Their fur color can vary from gray to golden-brown, with a creamy-white underside.

408.

Their large eyes give them excellent night vision, aiding in their nocturnal activities.

409.

Hazel dormice are primarily arboreal, meaning they spend most of their lives in trees and shrubs.

410.

They have a prehensile tail, which means they can use it to grasp onto branches and climb with ease.

411.

The dormice's diet mainly consists of fruits, flowers, and insects. They have a preference for hazelnuts, hence their name.

412.

During the summer and fall, they consume large amounts of food to build up fat reserves for hibernation.

413.

Hazel dormice are known for their ability to hibernate for long periods, sometimes up to seven months, during colder months.

414.

They build elaborate nests called dreys, usually made from leaves, twigs, and grass, high up in trees or shrubs.

415.

Dormice are solitary animals, and each individual typically has its own territory.

416.

Their territories can range from 0.5 to 1 hectare in size, depending on food availability.

417.

Hazel dormice communicate through vocalizations, including high-pitched calls and clicks.

418.

Mating occurs in the late spring or early summer, and females usually have one or two litters per year.

419.

The gestation period is around 24 to 26 days, and a typical litter size is three to five pups.

420.

Newborn dormice are blind, hairless, and entirely dependent on their mother for care.

421.

Mother dormice create a cozy nest for their young, providing warmth and protection.

422.

The mother's milk is rich in fat and protein, aiding the rapid growth of the pups.

423.

Young dormice start to venture out of the nest and explore their surroundings at about three weeks old.

424.

Hazel dormice have a lifespan of around two to five years in the wild.

425.

They face various threats, including habitat loss due to deforestation and fragmentation.

426.

In some regions, they are also vulnerable to predation by birds, snakes, and other small mammals.

427.

Conservation efforts are in place to protect the dormice's habitat and raise awareness about their importance in the ecosystem.

428.

They play a role in seed dispersal, helping to maintain healthy forest ecosystems.

429.

Hazel dormice are legally protected in many countries due to their declining populations.

430.

In captivity, they have been observed using their tails to carry nesting material and even food.

431.

These dormice have a unique defense mechanism called "torpor," where their body temperature drops significantly to conserve energy.

432.

Torpor is different from hibernation as it occurs for shorter durations and is more adaptive to changes in weather.

433.

Hazel dormice are agile climbers and can move gracefully through trees and bushes.

434.

Their strong hind limbs make them adept at jumping from branch to branch.

435.

Dormice are important indicators of the health of woodland ecosystems.

436.

The presence of Hazel Dormice in an area can signify the presence of diverse habitats with ample food sources.

437.

The dormouse population can be affected by climate change, which can alter the availability of their preferred foods.

438.

In some cultures, Hazel Dormice are considered a delicacy and are hunted for food.

439.

They have a gentle temperament and are not aggressive animals.

440.

The Hazel Dormouse has been featured in literature and folklore, often symbolizing qualities like gentleness and innocence.

441.

In the UK, hazel dormice are a protected species under the Wildlife and Countryside Act.

442.

Dormice are known to groom themselves meticulously, keeping their fur clean and well-groomed.

443.

Their ability to curl into a tight ball, with their bushy tail acting as a shield, helps them protect themselves from predators.

444.

Hazel dormice have a remarkable ability to find their way back to their home territory even after being displaced.

445.

The dormouse's activities play a crucial role in nutrient cycling and seed dispersal within their habitat.

446.

They are sensitive to temperature changes, and warmer winters can lead to premature emergence from hibernation, resulting in decreased survival rates.

447.

The IUCN lists the Hazel Dormouse as "Near Threatened" due to declining populations in some parts of its range.

448.

Efforts to monitor and conserve dormouse populations include the creation of wildlife corridors and protected reserves.

449.

Researchers use nest boxes to study and monitor dormouse populations in various regions.

450.

Observing the natural behaviors of Hazel Dormice can provide valuable insights into their role in maintaining healthy ecosystems and the broader impacts of environmental changes on wildlife.

451.

Hector's Dolphin is the smallest and one of the rarest dolphin species in the world.

452.

They are named after Sir James Hector, a prominent New Zealand scientist.

453.

There are two subspecies of Hector's Dolphin: the North Island Hector's Dolphin and the South Island Hector's Dolphin.

454.

They have distinctive rounded dorsal fins and a characteristic black facial marking that stretches from their dorsal fin to their rostrum.

455.

Hector's Dolphins are known for their striking coloration, which varies from light gray to slate gray, with a white underside.

456.

The North Island subspecies has a shorter snout and a more pronounced black eye patch compared to the South Island subspecies.

457.

They are often called "dolphins with a perm" due to their distinctive dorsal fin shape resembling a curly hairstyle.

458.

Hector's Dolphins are typically found close to the coast in shallow waters.

459.

They prefer coastal areas with rocky substrates and strong currents.

460.

Hector's Dolphins have a playful and curious nature, often approaching boats to ride on the bow waves.

461.

These dolphins are known for their acrobatic behavior, frequently leaping out of the water and performing flips.

462.

They are social animals and often travel in small groups known as pods.

463.

Pods of Hector's Dolphins can consist of just a few individuals to around 20 dolphins.

464.

The diet of Hector's Dolphins mainly consists of small fish and squid.

465.

They use echolocation, emitting high-frequency clicks, to locate and catch their prey.

466.

Hector's Dolphins have a relatively short lifespan, averaging around 20 years.

467.

Female Hector's Dolphins mature at around 7 to 9 years of age, while males mature a bit later.

468.

Breeding can occur throughout the year, but there is a peak in spring and summer.

469.

Gestation lasts for about 10 to 11 months, and calves are typically born in the summer months.

470.

Newborn calves are about 60-80 cm long and weigh around 8-10 kg.

471.

Mother dolphins are attentive caregivers and nurse their calves for several months.

472.

Hector's Dolphins are known for their slow reproductive rate, which makes them vulnerable to population decline.

473.

The main threats to Hector's Dolphins include accidental entanglement in fishing gear, habitat degradation, pollution, and vessel interactions.

474.

New Zealand has implemented strict protection measures for Hector's Dolphins, including restricted fishing zones and speed limits for boats in certain areas.

475.

The total population of Hector's Dolphins is estimated to be around 7,000 individuals.

476.

The South Island subspecies has a larger population compared to the North Island subspecies.

477.

The critically endangered Maui's Dolphin is a subspecies of Hector's Dolphin, found exclusively on the west coast of the North Island.

478.

The Maui's Dolphin population is estimated to be around 50 individuals, making it one of the rarest marine mammals on the planet.

479.

Conservation efforts are underway to protect and recover both Hector's and Maui's Dolphin populations.

480.

Research initiatives involve using photo-identification techniques to track and monitor individual dolphins over time.

481.

The New Zealand government has established marine protected areas to safeguard dolphin habitats.

482.

Tourist boat operators offer eco-friendly dolphin-watching tours to raise awareness and support conservation efforts.

483.

Hector's Dolphins have been studied extensively due to their unique features and vulnerability.

484.

Their geographic isolation has led to distinct genetic differences between the North and South Island populations.

485.

The endangered status of Hector's Dolphins has garnered attention and support from environmental organizations and researchers.

486.

The Māori name for Hector's Dolphin is "tutumairekurai."

487.

Hector's Dolphins play a vital role in New Zealand's marine ecosystem as both predators and prey.

488.

They contribute to the overall biodiversity and health of their coastal habitats.

489.

The Hector's Dolphin is the only dolphin species endemic to New Zealand waters.

490.

In 2008, the New Zealand government introduced a Threat Management Plan to address the conservation challenges facing Hector's and Maui's Dolphins.

491.

The Hector's Dolphin is featured on New Zealand's five-cent coin.

492.

While they are known for their playful behavior, the conservation of Hector's Dolphins is a serious concern.

493.

The Hector's Dolphin is a flagship species for marine conservation efforts in New Zealand.

494.

A significant portion of their habitat overlaps with human activities, making effective management strategies essential.

495.

The International Union for Conservation of Nature (IUCN) lists Hector's Dolphins as endangered.

496.

The survival of these dolphins is closely linked to sustainable fishing practices and reducing human impacts on their habitats.

497.

Hector's Dolphins are known for their curiosity towards humans and boats, often riding the bow waves.

498.

There are ongoing efforts to raise public awareness about the importance of protecting these iconic dolphins.

499.

The conservation of Hector's Dolphins reflects the broader need to preserve marine biodiversity and ensure the health of ocean ecosystems.

500.

The survival of Hector's Dolphins is a testament to the interconnectedness of species and the impact of human activities on fragile ecosystems.

501.

Campbell Soup Company, also known as Campbell's, was founded in 1869 by fruit merchant Joseph A. Campbell and icebox manufacturer Abraham Anderson.

502.

The company's first product was condensed tomato soup, introduced in 1897.

503.

The iconic red and white label of Campbell's soups was introduced in 1898.

504.

Campbell's famous "M'm! M'm! Good!" slogan was first used in 1935.

505.

In 1915, Campbell's introduced its first vegetable soup, making it the first company to offer condensed ready-to-eat soups.

506.

During World War II, Campbell's provided canned soups to the military, earning them the Army-Navy "E" Award for excellence in wartime production.

507.

Campbell's has expanded beyond soups to include a variety of food products, including sauces, pasta, snacks, and beverages.

508.

The company's headquarters is located in Camden, New Jersey, where it started.

509.

In 1954, Campbell's introduced its iconic chicken noodle soup, which became one of its most popular products.

510.

Andy Warhol's famous "Campbell's Soup Cans" artwork, created in 1962, immortalized the company's brand in the world of art.

511.

Campbell's introduced the "Chunky" line of soups in 1970, catering to those looking for heartier options.

512.

The Campbell Kids, a group of illustrated children, have been a part of the company's branding since the early 1900s.

513.

In 1981, Campbell's launched its "Soup at Hand" line, providing convenient single-serve soup cups.

514.

The company expanded its international presence through acquisitions and partnerships, entering markets worldwide.

515.

Campbell's introduced the "V8" line of vegetable juices in 1948, promoting healthy nutrition.

516.

In 1998, the Campbell Soup Company acquired the Prego pasta sauce brand.

517.

Campbell's has a rich history of community involvement and charitable initiatives.

518.

The company's commitment to sustainability led to efforts to reduce its environmental impact and promote responsible sourcing.

519.

In 2001, Campbell's introduced its "Select Harvest" line of soups, emphasizing natural ingredients and flavors.

520.

The Campbell Soup Foundation was established in 1953 to support community-based organizations.

521.

Campbell's has faced challenges and changes in consumer preferences, leading to a focus on innovation and healthier options.

522.

In 2012, the company introduced a new logo, modernizing its brand identity.

523.

Campbell's expanded into the organic market with the introduction of "Campbell's Organic" in 2015.

524.

The company acquired the Bolthouse Farms brand in 2012, which produces a range of beverages and fresh produce.

525.

Campbell's commitment to transparency and clean labels led to efforts to remove artificial ingredients from its products.

526.

In 2018, Campbell's acquired the snack company Snyder's-Lance, expanding its portfolio to include pretzels and chips.

527.

The "Well Yes!" line of soups, introduced in 2017, focuses on nutritious and wholesome ingredients.

528.

Campbell's has worked to address food insecurity through various initiatives and partnerships.

529.

The company's "Campbell's Go" line offers portable and microwavable soups for on-the-go consumers.

530.

In recent years, Campbell's has embraced e-commerce and direct-to-consumer channels to adapt to changing shopping habits.

531.

Campbell's commitment to diversity and inclusion is reflected in its workforce and initiatives.

532.

The company's corporate social responsibility efforts include sustainable sourcing, waste reduction, and community support.

533.

Campbell's introduced its "Wellness Wagon" initiative to provide fresh produce and nutrition education in underserved communities.

534.

The Campbell Soup Company established the "Nourish" program to promote healthy eating habits among children.

535.

Campbell's has experimented with limited-edition flavors and collaborations to appeal to a broader audience.

536.

The company's innovation lab, "The CAMP," focuses on developing new products and packaging concepts.

537.

Campbell's shifted its focus towards digital marketing and engagement to connect with consumers.

538.

The "Campbell's Kitchen" website offers a wide range of recipes using Campbell's products.

539.

The Campbell's Culinary & Baking Institute contributes to product development and culinary research.

540.

In 2021, Campbell's introduced a line of "Slow Kettle" soups, emphasizing premium ingredients and flavors.

541.

The company's sustainability efforts include reducing greenhouse gas emissions and water usage.

542.

Campbell's has made commitments to eliminate plastic packaging and transition to more sustainable alternatives.

543.

The company is known for supporting disaster relief efforts through product donations and financial contributions.

544.

Campbell's has a long history of advertising and marketing campaigns that have become embedded in popular culture.

545.

The "Campbell's Community Champion Awards" recognize employees who contribute to their communities.

546.

The company's presence extends to various social media platforms, engaging with consumers and sharing recipes.

547.

Campbell's participates in industry-wide efforts to address food waste and promote sustainable practices.

548.

The company's focus on innovation has led to the development of new products like plant-based soups and broths.

549.

Campbell's has been recognized for its efforts in promoting workplace diversity and equality.

550.

Despite evolving consumer preferences and market challenges, Campbell's remains an enduring symbol of comfort food and culinary tradition.

551.

The Clorox Company was founded in 1913 in Oakland, California, by five entrepreneurs: Archibald Taft, Edward Hughes, Charles Husband, Rufus Myers, and William Hussey.

552.

The company's first product was a liquid bleach called "Clorox Bleach," which was initially developed as a cleaning solution for industrial purposes.

553.

The name "Clorox" is a combination of the words "chlorine" and "sodium hydroxide," the main ingredients in bleach.

554.

Clorox bleach became widely recognized for its effectiveness in disinfecting and removing stains, making it a household staple.

555.

In 1922, Clorox introduced a powdered bleach that could be dissolved in water for convenient household use.

556.

Clorox bleach gained popularity during the 1918 flu pandemic when it was recommended as a disinfectant.

557.

The company's first bleach manufacturing plant was located in Oakland, California.

558.

Clorox was one of the first companies to develop and promote the use of bleach for laundry purposes, leading to its household popularity.

559.

In the early years, Clorox bleach was sold door-to-door by sales representatives.

560.

Clorox was one of the first companies to use direct mail advertising to promote its products to consumers.

561.

Clorox introduced its iconic diamond-shaped logo in 1957, symbolizing purity and strength.

562.

The Clorox Company went public in 1928, becoming publicly traded on the New York Stock Exchange.

563.

Clorox expanded its product portfolio beyond bleach, introducing a range of cleaning and disinfecting products for various applications.

564.

During World War II, Clorox provided bleach to the military for disinfection purposes.

565.

Clorox entered the international market, establishing its presence in Canada and other countries.

566.

The company's commitment to safety and quality led to the establishment of research and development facilities.

567.

Clorox introduced the first liquid bleach that could be used directly on colors without fading or damaging them.

568.

The company's emphasis on responsible manufacturing and environmental stewardship led to sustainability initiatives.

569.

Clorox acquired several brands over the years, expanding its product offerings in various categories.

570.

The company introduced its first concentrated bleach in the 1970s, allowing consumers to use less product for the same results.

571.

Clorox expanded into the healthcare industry, providing disinfecting solutions for hospitals and healthcare facilities.

572.

The Clorox Company acquired the Burt's Bees brand, known for natural personal care products, in 2007.

573.

Clorox launched its "Green Works" line of cleaning products, focusing on environmentally friendly ingredients.

574.

The company introduced disinfecting wipes in the 1990s, providing a convenient and effective way to clean and sanitize surfaces.

575.

Clorox has a history of philanthropy, supporting various social and community initiatives.

576.

The company's commitment to diversity and inclusion has been recognized through various awards and recognitions.

577.

Clorox's "Bleach It Away" campaign allowed consumers to share their personal stories of using Clorox products for cleaning challenges.

578.

The Clorox Company has consistently ranked on lists of the most ethical companies.

579.

Clorox introduced the "Smart Tube" technology, designed to ensure users can dispense every last drop of product from the bottle.

580.

The company has a commitment to reducing its environmental footprint, including greenhouse gas emissions and water usage.

581.

Clorox launched its "Ingredients Inside" program to provide transparency about the ingredients used in its products.

582.

The Clorox Company expanded its product offerings to include natural, eco-friendly alternatives to traditional cleaning products.

583.

The company's response to the COVID-19 pandemic included increasing production of disinfecting products to meet demand.

584.

Clorox's "Clean Spaces for All" initiative aimed to help create healthier and more welcoming communities.

585.

The Clorox Company has been recognized for its workplace diversity and inclusion efforts.

586.

The company's portfolio includes well-known brands like Pine-Sol, Glad, Brita, and Kingsford.

587.

Clorox has a history of collaborating with organizations to promote cleanliness, hygiene, and health education.

588.

The company introduced "Clorox 2" as a color-safe bleach alternative for fabrics.

589.

Clorox was among the first companies to use bleach for cleaning outdoor decks and patios.

590.

The Clorox Company established a partnership with DonorsChoose.org to support teachers and classrooms.

591.

Clorox has received recognition for its efforts in reducing plastic waste through sustainable packaging initiatives.

592.

The company's disinfecting products gained significant attention during the COVID-19 pandemic.

593.

Clorox's corporate social responsibility efforts include charitable donations, disaster relief, and community support.

594.

The company's commitment to public health and safety has made Clorox a trusted brand during times of crisis.

595.

Clorox has consistently adapted its products to meet changing consumer needs and preferences.

596.

The Clorox Company's corporate headquarters is located in Oakland, California.

597.

The company operates in more than 100 countries, with a global presence in the cleaning and consumer goods industry.

598.

Clorox has a history of investing in research and development to innovate and improve its products.

599.

The company's commitment to quality control ensures that its products meet rigorous safety and efficacy standards.

600.

Clorox's legacy as a pioneer in the cleaning and disinfecting industry continues to be felt in households worldwide.

601.

The Tapping Reeve House and Law School is located in Litchfield, Connecticut, and is considered one of the earliest and most influential law schools in the United States.

602.

The law school was founded by Tapping Reeve in 1784, making it the first law school in the country.

603.

Tapping Reeve was a prominent lawyer, educator, and jurist, known for his contributions to legal education and the practice of law.

604.

The law school operated from 1784 to 1833 and trained over 1,100 students during its years of operation.

605.

Tapping Reeve's innovative teaching methods emphasized practical application of the law and the Socratic method of instruction.

606.

Students of the law school came from various backgrounds and states, contributing to its reputation as a center of legal education.

607.

The law school's curriculum covered various legal subjects, including property law, contracts, torts, criminal law, and constitutional law.

608.

The Tapping Reeve House served as both the residence of Tapping Reeve and the classroom for the law school.

609.

The Tapping Reeve House is a Federal-style building with distinctive architectural features, such as a central chimney and symmetrical design.

610.

The Tapping Reeve House has been preserved as a historic site and museum, offering visitors insights into early legal education and daily life in the late 18th century.

611.

The Litchfield Law School was unique in its time for admitting both men and women as students, contributing to its inclusive reputation.

612.

One of the notable students of the law school was Aaron Burr, who later became the third Vice President of the United States.

613.

Another notable student was John C. Calhoun, who became the seventh Vice President and was known for his influential political career.

614.

The law school's reputation extended beyond legal education, as it also served as a social and intellectual hub for the community.

615.

Tapping Reeve's wife, Sally Reeve, played an active role in the law school's operations and contributed to its welcoming atmosphere.

616.

The law school's success and reputation led to the establishment of other law schools based on its model.

617.

Tapping Reeve's commitment to legal education and his dedication to improving the legal profession left a lasting impact on American jurisprudence.

618.

The law school's curriculum focused on the practical aspects of law practice, including the preparation of legal documents and courtroom procedures.

619.

Tapping Reeve was a strong advocate for legal reform and believed in the importance of well-educated lawyers in upholding the rule of law.

620.

The Tapping Reeve House and Law School is now operated by the Litchfield Historical Society and offers guided tours to visitors.

621.

The Tapping Reeve House is furnished with period-appropriate furniture, providing a glimpse into the daily life of the Reeve family.

622.

The Litchfield Law School attracted students from various states, including New York, Massachusetts, Vermont, and beyond.

623.

The law school's impact on legal education was significant, as its methods and curriculum influenced the development of law schools throughout the country.

624.

The Tapping Reeve House and Law School was designated a National Historic Landmark in 1965.

625.

The law school's legacy is celebrated through educational programs, lectures, and events organized by the Litchfield Historical Society.

626.

The law school's alumni went on to play important roles in various fields, including law, politics, business, and academia.

627.

The Litchfield Law School was unique in its approach to legal education, focusing on case-based learning and practical experience.

628.

The law school's students participated in moot courts, debates, and legal discussions to develop their advocacy and reasoning skills.

629.

Tapping Reeve's commitment to education extended beyond the law school, as he also founded the Litchfield Female Academy to provide education for women.

630.

The law school's archives and records provide valuable insights into legal education, student life, and early American legal practice.

631.

The Tapping Reeve House is preserved with its original architectural elements, showcasing the craftsmanship of the late 18th century.

632.

The law school's methods were considered groundbreaking for their emphasis on critical thinking and analysis of legal principles.

633.

Tapping Reeve's reputation as a scholar and legal practitioner attracted students from various regions seeking high-quality legal education.

634.

The law school's alumni network included lawyers who later became judges, legislators, and influential figures in American history.

635.

The Tapping Reeve House and Law School provides a tangible connection to the early days of legal education and the development of the legal profession in the United States.

636.

The law school's success inspired other legal educators to adopt its teaching methods and curriculum, contributing to the spread of legal education.

637.

The Tapping Reeve House features exhibits that highlight the life and legacy of Tapping Reeve, as well as the significance of the law school.

638.

The law school's location in Litchfield, Connecticut, made it accessible to students from different states, contributing to its diverse student body.

639.

Tapping Reeve's vision for legal education emphasized the importance of ethical conduct, professionalism, and the pursuit of justice.

640.

The Litchfield Law School operated during a critical period in American history, as the country was shaping its legal and political systems.

641.

The law school's archives include student notebooks, correspondence, and legal documents that provide insights into legal education and practice.

642.

Tapping Reeve's legacy as a legal educator and advocate for the rule of law continues to inspire those interested in law and history.

643.

The Tapping Reeve House and Law School is a popular destination for history enthusiasts, educators, and individuals interested in the evolution of legal education.

644.

The law school's contributions to legal education were recognized by legal scholars and educators who studied its methods and impact.

645.

The law school's approach to teaching law was influenced by Tapping Reeve's experiences as a lawyer and judge in Connecticut.

646.

The Tapping Reeve House and Law School complex includes historical structures that showcase different aspects of early American life and education.

647.

The law school's curriculum aimed to provide students with a well-rounded education in various legal topics to prepare them for diverse legal careers.

648.

The Litchfield Law School's location in a rural setting provided a conducive environment for focused study and contemplation.

649.

Tapping Reeve's dedication to providing quality legal education contributed to the law school's enduring reputation as a pioneer in legal instruction.

650.

The Tapping Reeve House and Law School stand as a testament to Tapping Reeve's vision for legal education and his impact on shaping the legal profession in the United States.

651.

The Frederic Remington House is located in Ogdensburg, New York, and was the childhood home of the renowned American artist Frederic Remington.

652.

Frederic Remington (1861-1909) was a prominent painter, illustrator, sculptor, and writer known for his depictions of the American West.

653.

The house is a National Historic Landmark and is also known as the "Remington Art Museum."

654.

Frederic Remington's father, Seth Pierre Remington, was a successful local businessman and newspaper editor.

655.

The house was built in 1810 and has undergone renovations and modifications over the years while retaining its historical character.

656.

The house's architectural style reflects the Federal style prevalent in the early 19th century.

657.

Frederic Remington spent his formative years in the house, where he developed an early interest in art and the outdoors.

658.

Remington's exposure to the local landscape, wildlife, and Native American culture during his childhood greatly influenced his later artistic works.

659.

The house is filled with original Remington family furnishings, offering a glimpse into the daily life of the artist's family.

660.

The Remington family occupied the house until 1876 when they moved to another residence in Ogdensburg.

661.

The house remained in private ownership until it was acquired by the Remington Museum in the 1920s.

662.

The Remington Art Museum was established in 1923 with the goal of preserving the legacy of Frederic Remington.

663.

The museum showcases a diverse collection of Remington's artwork, including paintings, sculptures, illustrations, and personal items.

664.

The Frederic Remington House is an important pilgrimage site for art enthusiasts and admirers of Western art.

665.

The house's preservation efforts have maintained its historical integrity, allowing visitors to experience the environment in which Remington grew up.

666.

In addition to Remington's works, the museum also features exhibitions by other artists and hosts educational programs and events.

667.

The museum's collection includes iconic Remington pieces like "Bronco Buster" and "Coming Through the Rye."

668.

The Frederic Remington House and Museum offer insights into the artist's creative process, his travels, and his exploration of the American West.

669.

The house is filled with artifacts, photographs, and memorabilia that provide a comprehensive view of Remington's life and career.

670.

The Remington Museum's mission is to educate visitors about the artist's contributions to American art and culture.

671.

The house's location near the St. Lawrence River reflects Remington's love for outdoor activities like hunting, fishing, and boating.

672.

The museum's exhibitions explore various aspects of Remington's artistry, including his portrayal of Western landscapes, Native Americans, and military scenes.

673.

The Remington Museum offers guided tours that delve into the artist's life, the historical context of his works, and his impact on American art.

674.

The Frederic Remington House is part of the Northern New York State Historic Sites system.

675.

The museum's collection includes sketches, paintings, sculptures, and personal letters that provide insights into Remington's artistic evolution.

676.

Remington's depictions of cowboys, soldiers, and frontier life became iconic images of the American West and contributed to the romanticization of the Wild West.

677.

The Remington Museum's outreach programs aim to engage students, teachers, and art enthusiasts in appreciating Remington's art and legacy.

678.

The museum collaborates with other cultural institutions to organize exhibitions and events that celebrate Western art and American heritage.

679.

Remington's illustrations and stories were published in prominent magazines of his time, contributing to his widespread recognition and fame.

680.

The Frederic Remington House and Museum serve as a hub for scholars and researchers studying Remington's art and its cultural significance.

681.

The museum's collection includes examples of Remington's work in various mediums, showcasing his versatility and artistic range.

682.

The museum hosts workshops, lectures, and art classes that allow participants to explore their creativity through Remington-inspired projects.

683.

The Remington Museum's curatorial team continually adds to the collection, ensuring that Remington's legacy remains relevant and vibrant.

684.

The Frederic Remington House and Museum have become a cultural center that promotes art appreciation, historical preservation, and community engagement.

685.

The museum's website provides virtual tours, educational resources, and information about upcoming exhibitions and events.

686.

The Frederic Remington House's location in upstate New York offers visitors the opportunity to explore the natural beauty of the region.

687.

The museum's dedication to preserving Remington's artistic legacy is reflected in its well-maintained facilities and exhibits.

688.

The Remington Museum's archives contain documents, photographs, and manuscripts that shed light on Remington's career and personal life.

689.

The museum's gift shop offers a range of merchandise inspired by Remington's artwork, including prints, books, and collectibles.

690.

The Frederic Remington House and Museum contribute to the cultural vibrancy of Ogdensburg and attract visitors from around the country.

691.

The museum's staff includes educators, curators, and volunteers who are passionate about sharing Remington's contributions to American art.

692.

Remington's commitment to accurately depicting the West led him to conduct research, study Native American cultures, and participate in frontier life.

693.

The Remington Museum's special events include art exhibitions, fundraising galas, and educational workshops for people of all ages.

694.

The museum's architecture and landscaping create a serene and inviting atmosphere that complements the artworks on display.

695.

The Frederic Remington House and Museum are dedicated to preserving Remington's connection to his hometown and celebrating his global impact.

696.

The museum's efforts to engage with local schools and colleges contribute to fostering an appreciation for art and history among young audiences.

697.

The Remington Museum's publications include catalogs, scholarly articles, and educational materials that contribute to the understanding of Remington's work.

698.

The Frederic Remington House serves as a tangible link to Remington's upbringing and influences, helping visitors understand the context of his art.

699.

The museum's commitment to accessibility is evident through its programs for visitors with disabilities and efforts to make the collection available online.

700.

The Frederic Remington House and Museum stand as a tribute to a visionary artist who captured the spirit of the American West and left an indelible mark on the art world.

701.

Hedgehogs are small nocturnal mammals belonging to the family Erinaceidae.

702.

They are characterized by their spiky, protective quills covering their backs and sides.

703.

Hedgehogs are found in Europe, Asia, Africa, and New Zealand, with different species inhabiting various regions.

704.

There are about 17 recognized species of hedgehogs.

705.

Hedgehogs have poor eyesight but possess excellent senses of smell and hearing.

706.

Their quills, made of modified hairs, serve as a defense mechanism against predators.

707.

When threatened, hedgehogs curl into a tight ball, protecting their vulnerable underside.

708.

Hedgehogs are insectivores, primarily consuming insects, worms, snails, and even small vertebrates.

709.

They have a unique behavior called "self-anointing," where they lick or chew on strong-smelling substances and then spread the frothy mixture on their quills.

710.

Hedgehogs are solitary animals and are mostly active during the night.

711.

They have a natural resistance to snake venom due to their consumption of venomous snakes and immunity-building behavior.

712.

Hedgehogs are known to hibernate during the colder months, lowering their body temperature and metabolic rate.

713.

Hibernation allows hedgehogs to conserve energy when food is scarce.

714.

Hedgehogs are beneficial for gardens and farms as they help control insect populations.

715.

Their lifespan varies depending on the species and environmental factors, but they generally live for 2 to 7 years in the wild.

716.

Hedgehogs are popular as pets in some parts of the world, but they require specialized care and habitats.

717.

The European hedgehog is one of the most well-known species, often depicted in literature and art.

718.

Baby hedgehogs are called "hoglets."

719.

Hedgehogs communicate using a combination of vocalizations, body language, and scent markings.

720.

In some cultures, hedgehogs are considered symbols of protection and resourcefulness.

721.

Hedgehogs can run at a speed of about 1.5 miles per hour.

722.

The hedgehog's scientific name is Erinaceus europaeus.

723.

They have a unique adaptation known as a "hedgehog's dilemma,"
where they struggle to balance their need for social interaction with
their desire to avoid harm from close contact.

724.

Hedgehogs have a relatively low body temperature compared to
other mammals.

725.

Their diet can vary depending on the availability of food, with
insects being their primary source of nutrition.

726.

Hedgehogs have a small tail that is often hidden beneath their quills.

727.

Their quills are not barbed or poisonous but are effective at deterring
predators.

728.

Hedgehogs are known to roll over on their backs to scratch their
quills against the ground, aiding in shedding old spines.

729.

They are known to consume small amounts of carrion or roadkill
when other food sources are scarce.

730.

The mating ritual of hedgehogs involves courtship displays, scent
marking, and vocalizations.

731.

A mother hedgehog is called a "sow," and a father is called a "boar."

732.

Hedgehogs have a relatively low reproductive rate, with litters typically ranging from one to eleven hoglets.

733.

The hoglets are born blind, with soft spines that harden within a few hours.

734.

Female hedgehogs may nurse their young for about three to four weeks before they are weaned.

735.

Hedgehogs have a natural immunity to certain toxins and venom, which allows them to consume various insects and even some poisonous creatures.

736.

Their spines are made of keratin, the same protein found in human hair and nails.

737.

Hedgehogs play a role in seed dispersal by consuming fruits and spreading the seeds in their droppings.

738.

In some countries, hedgehogs are considered a threatened or endangered species due to habitat loss and road mortality.

739.

Some hedgehog species are able to climb trees or swim when necessary.

740.

Hedgehogs have a strong homing instinct and are known to return to familiar areas.

741.

They have been featured in literature and folklore for centuries, often as characters in fables and stories.

742.

Hedgehogs' presence in gardens is considered a sign of a healthy ecosystem.

743.

Hedgehog populations are facing challenges such as habitat destruction, road accidents, and pesticide use affecting their food sources.

744.

Conservation efforts are underway in various countries to protect hedgehog habitats and raise awareness about their importance.

745.

Hedgehogs can cover long distances during their nightly foraging expeditions, searching for food.

746.

The famous video game character Sonic the Hedgehog is inspired by a blue anthropomorphic hedgehog.

747.

Hedgehogs are known to "click" when they are excited or curious.

748.

Some species of hedgehogs have the ability to change their coat color during different seasons.

749.

Hedgehogs have a specialized immunity system that prevents them from contracting certain diseases that affect other animals.

750.

Due to their unique appearance and behaviors, hedgehogs have captured the fascination of people worldwide and continue to be admired and studied.

751.

Hermit crabs are crustaceans belonging to the family Paguridae and are closely related to true crabs.

752.

They are known for their unique behavior of using empty seashells as protective homes.

753.

Hermit crabs do not grow their own shells; instead, they find and use discarded shells from other marine creatures.

754.

As hermit crabs grow, they need to find larger shells to accommodate their increasing size.

755.

Hermit crabs are found in oceans, seas, and coastal areas around the world.

756.

There are over 1,000 species of hermit crabs, and they vary in size from a fraction of an inch to several inches in length.

757.

The largest hermit crab species, the coconut crab, can grow up to 16 inches in length and weigh up to 9 pounds.

758.

Hermit crabs have a soft abdomen that they protect by residing in a shell.

759.

The abdomen of a hermit crab curls to fit snugly into the shell, leaving only its head, legs, and claws exposed.

760.

Hermit crabs have two pairs of antennae that they use for sensory perception and communication.

761.

The larger pair of antennae are used for touch and detecting odors, while the smaller pair are used for sensory input.

762.

Hermit crabs are omnivores, meaning they eat a variety of plant and animal matter, including algae, plankton, detritus, and small invertebrates.

763.

They use their small pincers to bring food to their mouths.

764.

Hermit crabs are scavengers, feeding on dead organisms and other organic material they find.

765.

Hermit crabs have specialized gills that allow them to extract oxygen from both water and air.

766.

Their gills need to be kept moist to function properly, which is why hermit crabs are usually found near water.

767.

Some hermit crab species have an interesting relationship with sea anemones. They use the stinging tentacles of sea anemones for protection against predators.

768.

The sea anemone benefits from the hermit crab's movement, which helps it find food.

769.

Hermit crabs communicate with each other using tactile signals and by producing sounds.

770.

Their sounds are created by rubbing different body parts together.

771.

Hermit crabs undergo molting, shedding their exoskeleton to grow larger. They then seek a new shell that fits their new size.

772.

Molting is a vulnerable period for hermit crabs, as their soft exoskeleton offers less protection.

773.

Hermit crabs often hide during molting to avoid predators.

774.

They are known to "gang up" on larger predators to protect themselves and their colony.

775.

Hermit crabs are social creatures and can live in groups, often referred to as "clusters" or "colonies."

776.

These clusters can include a variety of hermit crab species.

777.

In captivity, hermit crabs can be kept as pets, but they require proper care and an environment that mimics their natural habitat.

778.

Providing a variety of shell options is important for pet hermit crabs to find suitable homes as they grow.

779.

Hermit crabs are known to be curious creatures, exploring their surroundings and objects in their environment.

780.

Hermit crabs have a relatively short lifespan, usually around 3 to 6 years in the wild.

781.

Some species of hermit crabs are known for their bright colors and patterns.

782.

Hermit crabs have a good memory and can recognize familiar individuals and locations.

783.

They are known to be sensitive to changes in their environment, such as temperature and humidity.

784.

Hermit crabs are preyed upon by various animals, including birds, fish, octopuses, and larger crabs.

785.

The coconut crab is the largest terrestrial arthropod and is capable of climbing trees to feed on coconuts.

786.

Hermit crabs have evolved to fill various ecological niches, adapting to different types of environments and habitats.

787.

Their ecological role includes scavenging and nutrient recycling, contributing to the health of marine ecosystems.

788.

The blue-legged hermit crab, a popular pet, is often chosen for marine aquariums to help control algae growth.

789.

Some hermit crab species, like the Halloween hermit crab, have colorful and eye-catching appearance, making them popular in the aquarium trade.

790.

Hermit crabs are important for maintaining sand and sediment health in marine environments by aerating and turning over the substrate.

791.

Hermit crabs' presence on sandy beaches can prevent excessive algae growth and provide a natural balance.

792.

Hermit crabs are not typically aggressive towards each other, but they may compete for suitable shells.

793.

These crabs have a specialized grooming behavior in which they use their legs to clean their shell and limbs.

794.

Hermit crabs have specialized excretory organs called "green glands" that help eliminate waste and regulate their internal environment.

795.

Some hermit crab species, such as the strawberry hermit crab, have distinct patterns and colors on their exoskeleton.

796.

The strawberry hermit crab is known for its reddish body coloration, which resembles a strawberry.

797.

Hermit crabs play an important role in the marine food chain by consuming decaying matter and recycling nutrients.

798.

The process of selecting and changing shells is an integral part of a hermit crab's life, affecting its growth and survival.

799.

Hermit crabs have a relatively low reproductive rate, and females lay eggs that hatch into planktonic larvae.

800.

The early life stages of hermit crabs are particularly vulnerable to predation, which contributes to their lower survival rate.

801.

Eli Lilly and Company was founded on May 10, 1876, by Colonel Eli Lilly, a pharmaceutical chemist, in Indianapolis, Indiana, USA.

802.

Colonel Eli Lilly was committed to producing high-quality medicines and improving the pharmaceutical industry's standards.

803.

The company's first product was quinine, used to treat malaria, which was in high demand during the late 1800s.

804.

In its early years, the company also manufactured gelatin-coated pills, which were easier to swallow and quickly became popular.

805.

Eli Lilly played a significant role in early insulin production. In 1923, it collaborated with Canadian researchers to make insulin widely available to treat diabetes.

806.

During World War II, Eli Lilly contributed to the war effort by producing essential medicines and penicillin for soldiers.

807.

The company is known for pioneering the concept of research and development (R&D) in the pharmaceutical industry, investing in science to create innovative drugs.

808.

In the 1950s, Eli Lilly introduced methadone, a pain-relieving medication that became important for treating opioid addiction.

809.

The company's expansion extended globally, establishing subsidiaries and partnerships in various countries to distribute its products.

810.

Eli Lilly introduced Prozac (fluoxetine) in 1987, a groundbreaking antidepressant that revolutionized the treatment of depression.

811.

Prozac gained wide recognition as a "miracle pill" and became one of the most prescribed antidepressants globally.

812.

The introduction of Prozac marked the beginning of Eli Lilly's presence in the psychiatric medication field.

813.

In the 1990s, Eli Lilly developed Humulin, the first synthetic human insulin, which significantly improved insulin treatment for diabetes patients.

814.

The company's animal health division, Elanco, was established in 1954, providing veterinary products and services.

815.

Eli Lilly's commitment to philanthropy led to the creation of the Eli Lilly and Company Foundation, which supports education, healthcare, and community development.

816.

Eli Lilly's strong focus on R&D led to the development of treatments for cancer, cardiovascular diseases, diabetes, and other chronic conditions.

817.

The company established a biotechnology division, exploring new frontiers in drug discovery and development.

818.

In the 21st century, Eli Lilly became a leader in the development of monoclonal antibodies for cancer treatment and other diseases.

819.

Eli Lilly's dedication to patient care led to programs like "Lilly Cares," providing free or discounted medications to those in need.

820.

The company has faced legal challenges related to drug pricing, marketing practices, and potential side effects of its products.

821.

In 2001, Eli Lilly and Company launched Cialis (tadalafil), a popular medication for erectile dysfunction.

822.

The Lilly Oncology Pipeline focuses on developing innovative treatments for various types of cancer.

823.

Eli Lilly expanded its research efforts to include neuroscience, developing medications for Alzheimer's disease and other neurological disorders.

824.

The company's commitment to sustainability led to efforts to reduce its environmental impact and support global health initiatives.

825.

Eli Lilly's headquarters, Lilly Corporate Center, is located in Indianapolis, Indiana.

826.

The company's logo features an intertwined "E" and "L" that represents Eli Lilly's dedication to innovation and improvement.

827.

Eli Lilly has received numerous awards and recognitions for its contributions to science, healthcare, and patient advocacy.

828.

The Lilly Diabetes Solution Center provides personalized assistance to diabetes patients, helping them access medications and manage their condition.

829.

Eli Lilly has been involved in collaborations with academic institutions, research organizations, and other pharmaceutical companies to advance scientific knowledge.

830.

The company has faced patent expirations for some of its key drugs, leading to competition from generic versions.

831.

Eli Lilly's commitment to diversity and inclusion includes initiatives to promote gender equality and representation in leadership roles.

832.

The company has invested in digital health technologies and data analytics to enhance patient care and outcomes.

833.

Eli Lilly's revenue and global reach have made it one of the largest pharmaceutical companies in the world.

834.

The Lilly Endowment, Inc., a separate entity from the company, is one of the largest private foundations in the United States and supports education, community development, and religion.

835.

Eli Lilly has been recognized for its ethical business practices and commitment to transparency in clinical trials.

836.

The company's research and development efforts have led to the discovery and development of groundbreaking treatments for a range of diseases.

837.

Eli Lilly is actively engaged in initiatives to address global health challenges, including access to essential medicines in developing countries.

838.

The company's dedication to patient safety involves rigorous testing and monitoring of its products throughout their lifecycle.

839.

Eli Lilly's portfolio includes treatments for autoimmune diseases, osteoporosis, and other conditions affecting millions of people worldwide.

840.

The Lilly Innovation Center in Cambridge, Massachusetts, focuses on research in immunology, oncology, and neurodegenerative diseases.

841.

Eli Lilly's commitment to sustainability has led to investments in renewable energy, waste reduction, and eco-friendly manufacturing practices.

842.

The company has faced criticism and legal action related to the marketing and potential side effects of certain medications.

843.

Eli Lilly is known for its contributions to the development of innovative insulin delivery methods, such as insulin pens and pumps.

844.

The company's partnerships with patient advocacy organizations demonstrate its commitment to improving patients' lives beyond medications.

845.

Eli Lilly's presence extends to over 120 countries, making its medications accessible to people around the world.

846.

The company's drug development process involves rigorous testing to ensure safety and effectiveness.

847.

Eli Lilly's commitment to addressing unmet medical needs has led to research in areas with limited treatment options.

848.

The company's support for clinical trials and medical research has contributed to advancements in various fields of medicine.

849.

Eli Lilly continues to invest in technologies that enhance patient engagement and facilitate better health outcomes.

850.

The company's long history is characterized by a commitment to innovation, patient care, and scientific excellence.

851.

The Goodyear Tire & Rubber Company was founded on August 29, 1898, by Frank Seiberling in Akron, Ohio.

852.

The company is named after Charles Goodyear, who invented the vulcanization process that revolutionized the rubber industry.

853.

Goodyear produced its first bicycle tire in 1898 and its first automobile tire in 1901.

854.

In 1903, the company launched the first mass-produced tire, the Goodyear No. 1, which was white and had a diamond tread pattern.

855.

Goodyear played a significant role in World War I by supplying tires for airplanes, trucks, and other military vehicles.

856.

In 1927, Goodyear produced the world's first airplane tire, which was used on Charles Lindbergh's historic solo flight across the Atlantic.

857.

The company introduced the first all-weather tire, the "G3X," in 1934.

858.

Goodyear developed the first nylon tire in 1947, which was stronger and more durable than previous tires.

859.

In 1956, Goodyear introduced the first radial-ply tire for passenger cars, revolutionizing tire technology.

860.

The company's famous "Wingfoot" logo was introduced in 1900, symbolizing speed and progress.

861.

Goodyear's blimps have been a recognizable part of their branding and advertising efforts since 1925.

862.

The Goodyear Blimp is one of the most recognized advertising icons in the world.

863.

In 1960, Goodyear became the first tire company to use electronic computers to design and test tires.

864.

The company introduced the first all-season radial tire, the "Tiempo," in 1977.

865.

Goodyear's tires were used on the lunar roving vehicles during NASA's Apollo 15, 16, and 17 missions.

866.

The company introduced the first high-performance tire with aquachannel grooves, the "Aquasteel," in 1983.

867.

In 1986, Goodyear launched the "Eagle" line of performance tires, which became popular among sports car enthusiasts.

868.

Goodyear was the exclusive tire supplier for the NASCAR racing series from 1997 to 2022.

869.

The Goodyear blimp was used to cover major sporting events, including the Super Bowl and the Olympics.

870.

In 2003, Goodyear introduced the "RunOnFlat" tire technology, allowing drivers to continue driving for a limited distance after a puncture.

871.

Goodyear developed the "Assurance TripleTred" tire in 2004, which featured three distinct tread zones for different driving conditions.

872.

The company expanded its presence globally and established manufacturing facilities in various countries.

873.

In 2012, Goodyear introduced the "Fuel Max" line of tires designed to improve fuel efficiency.

874.

Goodyear developed the "Eagle F1 Supercar 3" tire for the Chevrolet Corvette Z06 in 2014.

875.

The company introduced the "Eagle 360" concept tire in 2016, featuring a spherical design for autonomous vehicles.

876.

Goodyear created the "Oxygene" concept tire in 2018, which used moss to generate oxygen through photosynthesis.

877.

The "ReCharge" concept tire, introduced in 2020, features a tread that can be replenished with capsules containing a customized liquid compound.

878.

Goodyear has been involved in various motorsports, including Formula One, endurance racing, and rally racing.

879.

The company's innovation centers focus on developing advanced tire materials, technologies, and sustainability solutions.

880.

Goodyear's "Air Maintenance Technology" allows tires to maintain optimal pressure through internal inflation systems.

881.

The "IntelliGrip Urban" concept tire, introduced in 2021, is designed for electric autonomous vehicles in urban settings.

882.

Goodyear has received numerous awards for its commitment to innovation, safety, and sustainability.

883.

The company has faced challenges, including competition from other tire manufacturers and shifts in consumer preferences.

884.

Goodyear has a history of supporting charitable initiatives and community engagement through its Goodyear Better Future program.

885.

The company has adapted to changing market demands, including the growing popularity of electric and autonomous vehicles.

886.

Goodyear's tires are used by a wide range of vehicles, from passenger cars to commercial trucks, airplanes, and off-road equipment.

887.

The Goodyear name is associated with quality, durability, and performance, making it a trusted brand among consumers.

888.

Goodyear has maintained a commitment to environmental sustainability through tire recycling, eco-friendly materials, and energy-efficient manufacturing.

889.

The company has invested in research to develop innovative tire technologies that enhance safety, performance, and longevity.

890.

Goodyear's tire innovations have contributed to improved handling, traction, and fuel efficiency for vehicles of all types.

891.

The company has a legacy of collaborating with automakers to design tires tailored to specific vehicle models.

892.

Goodyear's commitment to safety is evident in its tire technologies, such as RunOnFlat and winter tire options.

893.

The company actively engages in research and development to anticipate future trends and challenges in the automotive industry.

894.

Goodyear has faced market fluctuations and economic downturns but has remained a leading tire manufacturer.

895.

The company's dedication to providing quality tires and excellent customer service has contributed to its enduring success.

896.

Goodyear's products are used by millions of drivers around the world, impacting their safety and driving experience.

897.

The company's innovation efforts extend beyond tire design, encompassing digital solutions and mobility technologies.

898.

Goodyear's focus on sustainability includes efforts to reduce waste, conserve resources, and minimize its environmental footprint.

899.

The company's tire testing facilities are state-of-the-art, simulating various road and weather conditions for accurate evaluations.

900.

Goodyear continues to evolve with the automotive industry, seeking new ways to enhance mobility, safety, and overall driving experiences.

901.

John Rogers was born on October 30, 1829, in Salem, Massachusetts.

902.

He initially pursued a career in business and banking but later turned to sculpture as his true passion.

903.

Rogers studied art in Europe, including in Paris and Florence, to refine his sculpting skills.

904.

In 1859, Rogers opened his own studio in New York City, where he began producing his renowned "Rogers Groups."

905.

"Rogers Groups" were small, mass-produced plaster sculptures depicting scenes from everyday life, often with a touch of humor or social commentary.

906.

Rogers' sculptures were affordable and accessible to the middle class, making them popular household decorations in the late 19th century.

907.

He created over 80 different models of "Rogers Groups," covering a wide range of themes from family life to politics and the Civil War.

908.

"Checkers Up at the Farm" was one of Rogers' most famous sculptures, depicting a young boy teaching his dog to play checkers.

909.

Another well-known piece is "The Slave Auction," which portrayed the injustice of the slave trade and was a commentary on the Civil War.

910.

Rogers was an astute observer of social issues, and his sculptures often provided a glimpse into the cultural and political climate of his time.

911.

His works were cast in plaster, making them more affordable than bronze sculptures, which allowed them to reach a broader audience.

912.

Rogers' attention to detail and realistic portrayal of human emotions set his sculptures apart from other contemporary works.

913.

He was known for his meticulous research and accuracy in depicting period clothing, furniture, and settings in his sculptures.

914.

Each "Rogers Group" was cast from a plaster mold, and the molds were destroyed after a certain number of casts were made, adding to their rarity.

915.

Rogers collaborated with art dealers to distribute his sculptures across the United States, leading to their widespread popularity.

916.

Despite their popularity, Rogers' sculptures were not always well-received by art critics, who sometimes dismissed them as "kitsch."

917.

Rogers' work faced criticism for its sentimentalism and perceived lack of artistic depth, but he remained dedicated to his craft.

918.

He continued to produce new sculptures throughout his career, responding to changing tastes and cultural shifts.

919.

The Rogers Group of sculptures declined in popularity with the rise of modernism in the early 20th century.

920.

In 1893, Rogers' studio was severely damaged in a fire, which led to the loss of many of his plaster molds.

921.

After the fire, Rogers focused on creating larger, more ambitious sculptures in bronze, moving away from the mass-produced "Rogers Groups."

922.

Rogers' bronze sculptures often depicted historical figures, Native American themes, and allegorical subjects.

923.

Despite his shift to bronze sculptures, his "Rogers Groups" remain his most iconic and enduring legacy.

924.

Rogers was a prolific artist, and his sculptures are now sought after by collectors and museums.

925.

His works are held in various museum collections, including the Metropolitan Museum of Art and the Smithsonian American Art Museum.

926.

The American Civil War greatly influenced Rogers' work, and many of his sculptures addressed the war's impact on families and society.

927.

"Union Refugees on the Way to Richmond" depicted a family of African American refugees fleeing the war's devastation.

928.

Rogers' sculptures often reflected his strong moral and social convictions.

929.

He was a member of several prominent art organizations, including the National Academy of Design.

930.

In 1896, Rogers was elected as an associate member of the National Academy of Design.

931.

Rogers continued to sculpt until his health declined, and he passed away on July 26, 1904, in New Canaan, Connecticut.

932.

After his death, interest in Rogers' sculptures waned, but there has been a renewed appreciation for his work in recent years.

933.

The John Rogers Sculpture Group, a nonprofit organization, was established to promote and preserve his legacy.

934.

The New York Historical Society organized a major exhibition of Rogers' work in 2009, bringing attention back to his contributions.

935.

Many of Rogers' sculptures are displayed in historical homes and museums across the United States.

936.

His ability to capture everyday moments with empathy and humor made his sculptures relatable to people of all backgrounds.

937.

The popularity of "Rogers Groups" in the 19th century reflects a broader shift in art consumption, as art became more accessible to the middle class.

938.

Rogers' sculptures offer a valuable glimpse into the domestic life, social values, and cultural norms of the 19th century.

939.

His attention to facial expressions and body language in his sculptures conveyed intricate narratives and emotions.

940.

Despite the criticism he faced, Rogers' work played a significant role in shaping American visual culture.

941.

Rogers' legacy extends beyond his art; his commitment to making art accessible to a wider audience set a precedent for later artists.

942.

His sculptures provide insight into the diverse experiences and perspectives of people during a transformative period in American history.

943.

"Rogers Groups" can still be found in antique shops, auction houses, and private collections.

944.

Collectors and enthusiasts of American art value Rogers' sculptures for their historical significance and artistic merit.

945.

The mass production of "Rogers Groups" marked a departure from the traditional model of art as a luxury for the elite.

946.

Rogers' sculptures served as a visual record of the daily lives, struggles, and joys of ordinary people.

947.

His work resonated with people who could see their own experiences reflected in his art.

948.

Rogers' sculptures can evoke a sense of nostalgia for a bygone era, offering a window into a world that existed over a century ago.

949.

His artistic contributions highlight the power of art to connect people across time and space.

950.

John Rogers' ability to capture the essence of human nature and social dynamics in his sculptures makes his work relevant and thought-provoking even in the present day.

951.

The Samuel Wadsworth Russell House was built in 1828-1830 and is considered a prime example of Greek Revival architecture in the United States.

952.

The mansion was designed by the renowned architect David Hoadley, who incorporated elements of the Greek Revival style, characterized by its symmetry and classical motifs.

953.

The house was commissioned by Samuel Wadsworth Russell, a prominent merchant, and banker in Middletown.

954.

The mansion was constructed using brownstone quarried from nearby Portland, Connecticut, giving it its distinctive reddish-brown color.

955.

The exterior of the house features iconic Greek Revival details such as columns, pilasters, and a pedimented gable.

956.

The Russell House is a two-and-a-half-story structure with a central entrance and a balanced facade.

957.

The house boasts an impressive portico with four massive Ionic columns supporting the pediment.

958.

The interior of the mansion features high ceilings, elaborate moldings, and decorative plasterwork, typical of the Greek Revival style.

959.

The entry hall is particularly noteworthy, featuring a stunning elliptical staircase with a domed skylight above.

960.

The first floor of the mansion includes a formal parlor, dining room, and sitting room, all adorned with period-appropriate furnishings and decor.

961.

The Russell House is notable for its transitional design elements, blending Federal-style architecture with the emerging Greek Revival style.

962.

The house remained in the Russell family until 1937 when it was sold to Wesleyan University.

963.

In 1938, the Russell House became the home of the Wesleyan University President's residence, a role it continues to serve today.

964.

The mansion was designated a National Historic Landmark in 2001, recognizing its architectural significance.

965.

Visitors can explore the interior of the house, taking guided tours to learn about its history, architecture, and the Russell family.

966.

The Samuel Wadsworth Russell House is open to the public and offers insights into the lifestyle of a wealthy 19th-century family.

967.

The house is often used as a venue for various events, lectures, and exhibitions related to history, art, and culture.

968.

The Russell family was involved in various industries, including banking, manufacturing, and shipping.

969.

Samuel Wadsworth Russell was a member of one of Connecticut's wealthiest families, allowing him to build the grand mansion.

970.

The mansion was constructed during a period of economic growth and architectural innovation in Middletown.

971.

The Greek Revival style gained popularity in the early 19th century as a reflection of classical ideals and democratic values.

972.

The Samuel Wadsworth Russell House is surrounded by beautifully landscaped gardens and lawns.

973.

The interior decoration of the house combines neoclassical elements with Victorian influences.

974.

The house's architectural significance lies in its successful incorporation of Greek Revival elements within a Federal-style framework.

975.

The Russell House is an example of the cultural and architectural connections between Connecticut and New York City during the 19th century.

976.

The mansion's location on High Street places it within a historic district that showcases a variety of architectural styles.

977.

The Russell family was active in community affairs, contributing to the social and cultural life of Middletown.

978.

The mansion's period rooms feature original furnishings, artwork, and artifacts from the 19th century.

979.

The Greek Revival architectural movement was inspired by ancient Greek temples and ideals of democracy and classical learning.

980.

The mansion's design includes elements of proportion, symmetry, and order characteristic of the Greek architectural style.

981.

The Russell House offers guided tours that explore the history of the family, the architecture, and the cultural context of the era.

982.

The Samuel Wadsworth Russell House provides a glimpse into the opulent lifestyle of an affluent family in the 19th century.

983.

The architecture of the house showcases the transition from earlier Federal-style aesthetics to the more assertive Greek Revival style.

984.

The mansion's design embodies the ideals of the time, reflecting cultural values and aspirations of the early 19th century.

985.

Visitors to the house can experience the grandeur and elegance of a bygone era through its architecture and furnishings.

986.

The mansion's significance extends beyond its architectural merit to its role as a repository of historical memory.

987.

The Samuel Wadsworth Russell House serves as a visual testament to the evolution of architectural tastes and styles in America.

988.

The Greek Revival style symbolized an interest in democratic ideals, classical knowledge, and the nation's cultural heritage.

989.

The Russell House has been meticulously preserved, allowing visitors to step back in time and experience the ambiance of the past.

990.

The mansion's connection to Wesleyan University emphasizes its continued importance as an educational and cultural resource.

991.

The Samuel Wadsworth Russell House showcases the intersection of architecture, history, and culture in the 19th century.

992.

The mansion's design elements, such as the portico and pilasters, are reminiscent of ancient Greek temples.

993.

The interior features original woodwork, decorative plaster, and period-appropriate furnishings that transport visitors to the early 1800s.

994.

The Russell House stands as a reminder of the craftsmanship and attention to detail that characterized 19th-century architecture.

995.

The house's preservation is a testament to the efforts of historic preservationists, scholars, and the local community.

996.

The architectural features of the mansion, including the columns and pediment, reflect the grandeur associated with Greek temples.

997.

The Samuel Wadsworth Russell House provides insights into the aspirations and tastes of the American elite in the 19th century.

998.

The mansion's architecture serves as a representation of the broader cultural exchange between the United States and Europe.

999.

The Russell House's historical and architectural significance contributes to Middletown's status as a city rich in heritage.

1000.

By preserving and sharing the story of the Russell family and their house, the mansion continues to inspire and educate visitors about the past.